Sad about Sammy

A Family Resource for Children
Experiencing Sibling Loss and Grief

Valette Sopp and **Tonya Southwick**
Illustrations by **Tonya Southwick**

Text copyright ©2014 by Tonya Southwick

Illustration copyright ©2014 by Tonya Southwick

All rights reserved. No part of this book may be reproduced or transmitted by any means whatsoever, either mechanical or electronic, without written permission from the publisher, except for brief excerpts quoted in a review.

Published by Southwick Press, 300 West Spring Street, Unit 702, Columbus Ohio 43215.

Printed by CreateSpace, An Amazon.com Company.

Extensive research and efforts were applied to provide the most complete care and information for the reader. The publisher however makes no warranty, expressed or implied within with respect to the material contained herein.

Written by Valette Sopp and Tonya Southwick

Illustrations including cover illustration by Tonya Southwick

Graphic Design including cover by Scott Southwick

Illustration photography and photography editing by Scott Southwick

Library of Congress Cataloging – in-Publication Data

Sopp, Valette

Southwick, Tonya

Summary: A family resource for children coping with sibling grief.

ISBN 1499278837

This book is dedicated to the loving memory of my precious daughter,
Stephanie Lauren.
Through your death I learned so much about life.
I love you dearly and miss you always.

I would like to express my sincere and heartfelt gratitude to my husband Glenn, our children Scott, David and Alena, our family and dear friends. You mean the world to me and have given a great gift through your generous support and encouragement. It is with your help this project came to completion.

With all my love,
Tonya

Introduction

Please allow me to express my deepest condolences to you for the loss of your child. I also suffered the devastating loss of my child. Stephanie, my second born, died when she was six weeks old due to complications following surgery to repair congenital heart defects. This was by far the most painful experience of my life. With my heart freshly shattered and feeling utterly overwhelmed, I searched for words to explain this seemingly impossible reality to my young son. Finding very little immediate help, my husband and I forged through the agonizing task on our own.

This book is intended to provide practical information to help you begin navigating your child's journey through sibling grief. While not a complete guide, it may be used as a tool to help you and your child open the door to frank discussion about death and the emotional experiences naturally following your shared loss.

My hope is that you will begin working through the grief process in a mutually beneficial way. The simple fact you are reading this book is indicative of your parental love and concern for the emotional well-being of your surviving child.

Please try to remember that grieving is a process, not an event. Each person travels through that process in their own unique way. Given the gifts of your patience, understanding, love and support, your child will begin moving forward through the process. Illustrations included in this book show passing seasonal changes, viewed through the window of the child's world, representing his/her emotional transitions. Reading this book together, perhaps many times over, may bring a sense of comfort and hope.

Emotional and physical wounds heal similarly; one layer after another, benefiting from gentle care and passage of time. The often-used adage, 'time heals all wounds', is not entirely accurate. What you do with that passage of time will greatly impact how healthy the end result will be. To be certain, you and your surviving child will carry an emotional scar, but it need not become a wound involving long-term difficulties.

Parents and children alike grieve. Family dynamics naturally change following the death of a child. Everyone wishes things could just return to the way they were before the tragedy, but of course this is impossible. You are forever changed and so are your other children.

My deepest desire is to provide support to you through this book as you move through the delicate process of grieving together and as you begin establishing a 'new normal' for your family.

May God bless you and your family during this very difficult time.

**Mommy and Daddy are home!
I was waiting for a long time.**

Parent Notes:

Your child will sense your mood and distress. Don't keep him guessing for too long. Many times a child's imagination provides him with frightening possibilities.

It is okay for your child to see you cry. Crying is a natural part of grief and can be beneficial.

Something is wrong.
Mommy is crying.

Uh-oh!
Am I in trouble?

Parent Notes:

Finality is a difficult concept for young children to grasp. Your child may repeatedly ask where the lost sibling has gone. Try to be patient with these repetitive questions, realizing your answers will help your surviving child process this difficult concept.

Simply speaking the word 'dead' or 'died' is difficult, but it will help your child's understanding. Try to avoid using vague phrases such as 'passed-away' and 'not with us anymore', as this can cause confusion especially for younger children.

Mommy hugs me tight.
Daddy says, "Sammy is dead."
"What does dead mean?" I ask.

Parent Notes:

Try to answer your child's questions honestly, but keep it simple. Keep in mind that young children process only a little at a time. When you answer questions, don't hurry to 'fill-in' the conversation. Allowing your discussion to move at a slower pace may give you more insight.

It is normal for children to ask about the sibling's belongings or make other comments that may seem inappropriate. This is part of processing information that is completely new to them. They may also turn to silly play to release those emotions. To see children happily playing soon after a tragic event is not a sign that they don't care.

Many children will 'play dead'. Playfully acting out stressful situations allows them to feel a sense of control in situations where they feel vulnerable or out of control.

**Dad says Sammy's heart doesn't go
　'bump, bump, bump,'
and there's no breathing in and out.**

　　　　　"Can the doctor make it all better?" I ask.
　　　　　　　"No. Sammy is gone."

　　　　　　　　　　"Will Sammy come home?"
　　　　　　　　　　"No honey."　"WHY?"

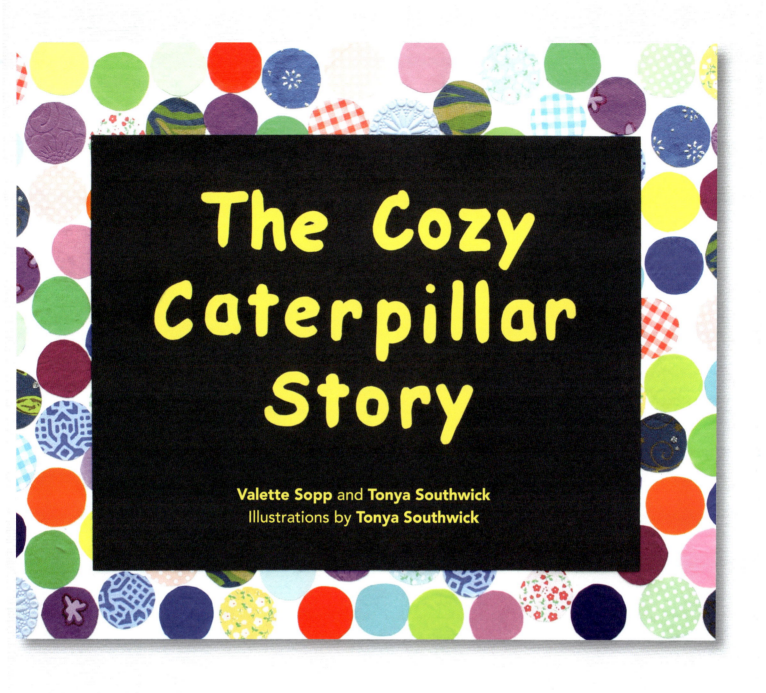

The Cozy Caterpillar Story

Valette Sopp and **Tonya Southwick**
Illustrations by **Tonya Southwick**

Mom reads this book to help me understand about Sammy.

Once there was a happy caterpillar family.
There was Papa Cozy, Mama Cozy; and their children,
Timmy, Tara, Tommy and Tiny. The Cozys always
stayed together. They wiggled and squiggled;
they climbed and played and stayed together.

One sad day, the Cozy caterpillar family
found that Tiny was gone.
All they could see was Tiny's empty shell.

Tiny's shell did not wiggle or squiggle.
Tiny's shell did not climb or play.

The Cozys missed Tiny and they were very sad.

They stopped wiggling and squiggling.

They stopped climbing and playing.

All they could do was carry around
Tiny's empty shell and cry, cry, cry.

One sunny day, Mama heard a quiet fluttering above. She put down Tiny's shell, looked up into the sky and saw the most beautiful butterfly. With a little squint of her eye, Mama could see Tiny's face! That beautiful butterfly was Tiny!

Look up, LOOK UP, LOOK UP!" Mama shouted. But Tiny's shell was so heavy the Cozy family could not look up.

"LOOK UP, LOOK UP!" Mama shouted again.

The Cozy family put Tiny's shell down and looked up.

Now the Cozys could see why Tiny could not wiggle and squiggle, or climb and play with them.

Together they watched as Tiny danced through
the clear blue sky!

And someday, they too would become beautiful butterflies,
dancing, flying and playing on the wind.

Parent Notes:

Ask your child, "What do you think the child in this picture is thinking about?" Or "Is there anything you want to talk about?" Either question will offer the opportunity to express thoughts or emotions.

This is a good time to talk with your child about your faith and what happens when someone dies.

As an added note, studies show that many children (especially boys) talk more openly when they are active. You may try talking while coloring or building blocks together instead of sitting down to talk.

Parent Notes:

You may wish to talk with your child's teachers and keep them informed about changes in your child's behavior or changes at home (relatives visiting, etc.).

The teacher will likely see behavioral changes at school. Some children may retreat or exhibit aggressive behavior. Allow the school to be a part of your child's compassionate support group.

Consistency in discipline and routine are important. Discipline may be especially difficult for you at this time; however a child's negative behavior may be his way of asking if he is still safe within the boundaries you have set.

I told my friend Sammy died.
He didn't say anything, so we just played.

Parent Notes:

Seeing photos may bring comfort or encourage discussion.

Holidays and other 'firsts' following the death of your child will be difficult for you. You may wish to limit your activities to only those that bring you comfort.

You may want to temporarily change some traditions. For example, share your meal with someone who may be alone, such as a senior citizen or neighbor. Or your might deliver treats to your local fire or police station or to another local charity. Remember to keep in mind the needs of your surviving child as you make these changes.

I see pictures of Sammy in my house.
I remember and I miss Sammy.

Parent Notes:

Young children are very egocentric; believing themselves to be at the center of all events. They may believe they caused this tragedy simply by wishing they didn't have a brother or sister. They may also think something they said caused their sibling to 'go away'.

Although it may not be a concern for your child, if you sense they are struggling with feelings of guilt, simply assure them they are not at fault.

I told Grandma that one time I got mad and wished Sammy would go away and never come back. But I didn't mean it.

Grandma said it is not my fault. Everyone gets mad sometimes, but angry feelings do not make people die.

Parent Notes:

Children interpret events through us. To help your child understand your tears, remind them of a time they cried but felt better later.

You may need to seek help from a professional counselor if you notice a definite shift from your child's usual behavior that does not go away on its own. Symptoms of depression may include the following: change in appetite, schoolwork, sleeping patterns, long term patterns of misbehavior or withdrawal from previously enjoyed activities. If you think your child may be depressed, ask your school counselor, clergy or pediatrician to recommend a professional counselor trained to help children.

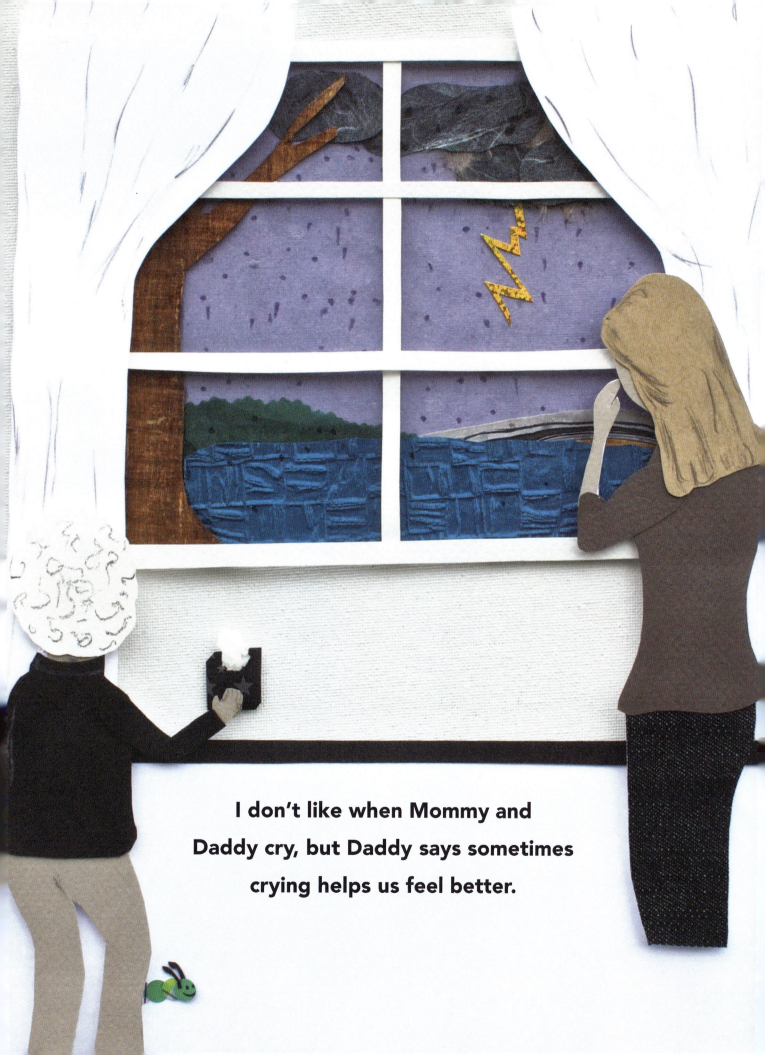

I don't like when Mommy and Daddy cry, but Daddy says sometimes crying helps us feel better.

Parent Notes:

Grieving the loss of your child can be all consuming. Try to share meaningful moments with your child that do not center on your grief. Make attempts to return to laughter and play. It is healthy for all involved if you take 'breaks' from grieving. You might go to the library or to the zoo. Consider volunteering together, playing games, watching a family movie with a big bowl of popcorn, or taking a walk.

Sometimes I think about what would happen to me if my mommy or daddy dies. Daddy says that most people get very old with lots of wrinkly skin before they die. He says we will probably all live for a very long time.

Parent Notes:

Allow children to help you and to feel useful during your grief. Even if they just bring a tissue for your tears, it will make them feel they have helped and that they are an important part of this ongoing healing process.

Help your child find ways to cope with the emotional changes in your family. Some suggestions are:

___ Pray.

___ Attend services at your place of worship.

___ Care for a pet.

___ Join a new club or class.

___ Volunteer.

___ Write a letter to their lost sibling.

___ Draw or paint.

___ Make a memory journal or keep a diary.

___ Hike.

___ Try a new sport.

___ Remind them to climb trees, run, play with friends, and to have fun.

It has been a long time since Sammy died. Mommy doesn't cry as much now.

Parent Notes:

A memorial for your deceased child can be a wonderful expression of your love for him. There are many ways you can create a memorial. Choose one that feels right for your family. You may wish to discuss different possibilities together before deciding what feels most comfortable.

Here are a few ideas you may consider:

___ Light a memorial candle.

___ Plant a tree or a living Christmas tree to decorate outdoors.

___ Make a donation to a selected charity.

___ Hang a special ornament on your Christmas tree.

___ Have a family portrait made by an artist capable of combining photos of each family member into one portrait.

___ Enter a race or walk-a-thon.

___ Commit to an annual family activity such as serving meals to homeless.

___ Sing songs or carols at a nursing home.

___ Give a gift to a child in need on your child's birthday.

Today we planted a tree to remember Sammy.
I helped dig a hole. Then I got to make it muddy with water.
Dad put a tree in and I patted new dirt on top.
I like to look at the tree and remember Sammy.

About the Authors:

Valette Sopp received her Bachelor of Science in Human Ecology and Child Development from The Ohio State University. She worked with the University in developing their Child Development Field Experience, and has supervised students within that program. She has worked with and been a teacher of young children for seventeen years. Enjoying artistic pursuits, Valette also enjoys painting murals for homes and businesses and currently resides with her husband in Ohio.

Tonya Southwick lost her second child, Stephanie, during infancy due to congenital heart defects. She enjoys a full life with her husband, three surviving children, family and friends. Currently residing in Ohio, Tonya enjoys outdoor activities, volunteering, and exploring the arts in her free time.

Acknowledgments:

Alena Southwick, illustrative art collaboration.

Scott Southwick, photography, photographic editing and graphic design.

Alex Gregory, editor.

Made in the USA
Charleston, SC
02 October 2014